Let Your Light Shine

For my grandchildren: May you always feel and share
the Savior's light.—B.C.

To my family: You're my heroes and my cheerleaders.
Thank you for your support and love!—C.N.

Text © 2022 Bonnie H. Cordon
Illustrations © 2022 Casey Nelson

All rights reserved. No part of this book may be reproduced in any form or by any means without permission in writing from the publisher, Deseret Book Company, at permissions@deseretbook.com. This work is not an official publication of The Church of Jesus Christ of Latter-day Saints. The views expressed herein are the responsibility of the author and do not necessarily represent the position of the Church or of Deseret Book Company.

Deseret Book is a registered trademark of Deseret Book Company.

Visit us at deseretbook.com

Library of Congress Cataloging-in-Publication Data
CIP data on file
ISBN 978-1-63993-063-0

Printed in China
RR Donnelley, Dongguan, China 4/2022

10 9 8 7 6 5 4 3 2 1

Let Your Light Shine

Written by
Bonnie H. Cordon

Illustrated by
Casey Nelson

DESERET
BOOK

Bonnie was so excited. She skipped across the field to the chicken coop and leaped over the little irrigation ditch that brought water to the corn and wheat.

Feeding the chickens was one of Bonnie's jobs on the family farm.

She didn't like it when the hungry birds squawked and pecked at her, but today she barely noticed. "Settle down!" she told the chickens. "Don't you know Elder Perry is coming tomorrow?" An Apostle of the Lord Jesus Christ was visiting their small town that weekend—and he was staying at her home!

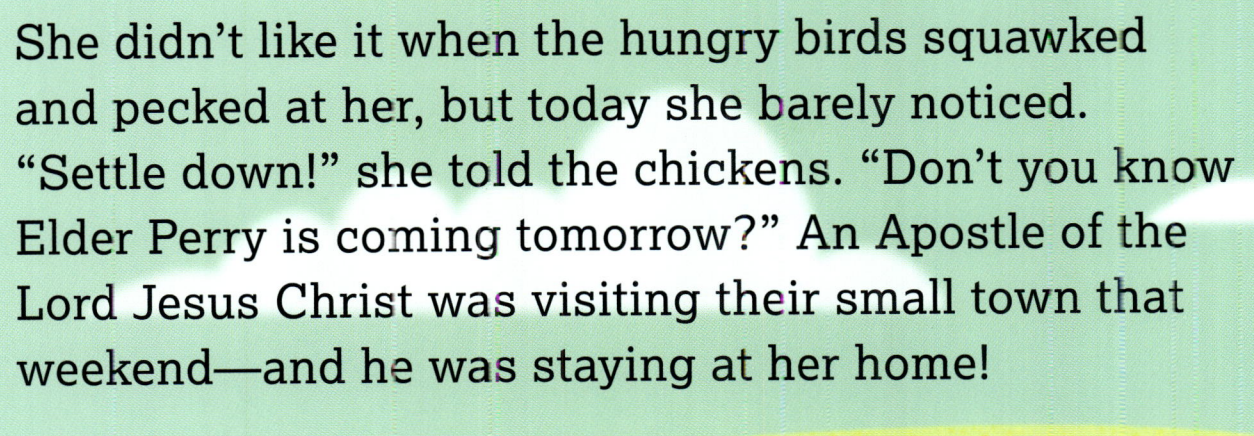

The next day, Bonnie hurried to help her family get everything ready for their special visitor. She helped Mother fix a delicious dinner, including homemade apple pie for dessert. The whole kitchen was soon filled with a cinnamon-sweet scent.

When Elder Perry arrived with his son, Bonnie was a little nervous. What would an Apostle be like?

But Elder Perry was so kind and cheerful, Bonnie soon felt completely comfortable.

After dinner, they sat down in the living room with big slices of apple pie. Bonnie was having such a wonderful time listening to Elder Perry's stories that she almost didn't hear her mother calling her from the kitchen.

With a sigh, Bonnie got to her feet and went into the kitchen. "Did you feed the chickens today, Bonnie?" asked her mother.

Oh no! In all the excitement, Bonnie had forgotten. Now she would have to make her way to the chicken coop in the dark. Even worse—she would miss Elder Perry's stories!

Bonnie's heart sank because she was afraid of the dark. She asked her brother if he would come with her. "No!" he said.

Just then she heard Elder Perry's cheerful voice, "Did I hear someone needs to feed the chickens? Can my son and I join you?"

Bonnie could hardly believe her ears! Suddenly, feeding the chickens was the most exciting thing she could imagine. She ran to get the large yellow flashlight and was soon leading the way across the fields.

Bonnie had just jumped across the irrigation ditch when she heard a SPLASH and a loud groan behind her. Disaster!

Elder Perry couldn't see the ditch in the dark, and he had stepped right into it! Bonnie turned the flashlight around and saw him shaking big drops of water from his heavy leather shoe. She felt terrible!

Elder Perry wasn't angry, though. Even though his foot was sloshing in the wet shoe, he kept on working until all the chickens were fed.

"Bonnie," Elder Perry said kindly as they turned back to the house, "I need to see the path. I need the light to shine where I am walking." Bonnie nodded as he smiled and shook out his wet shoe once more.

On the way back, Bonnie held the flashlight steady and aimed it carefully at the path right in front of Elder Perry. They were soon home safely—and with no more wet feet.

Bonnie thought about what she had learned later that night. She knew that the scriptures tell us, "Let your light so shine." Now she understood *why* we shine our light: to help others see the path.

"I am the light which ye shall hold up," Jesus said.

Bonnie never forgot the lesson she had learned about holding up the Savior's light.

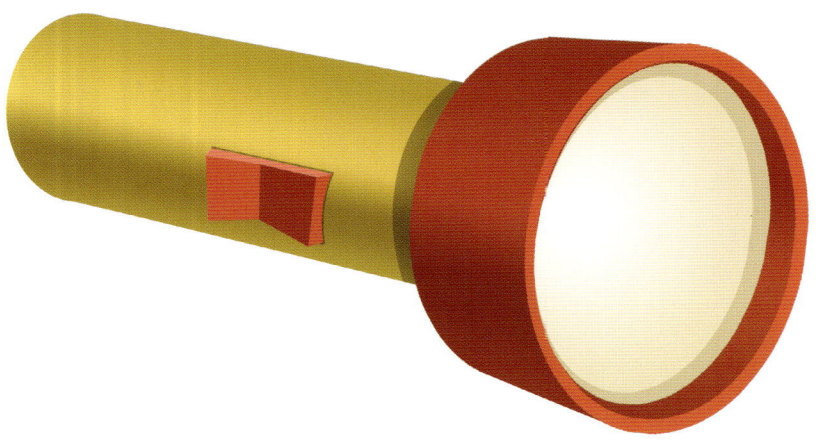

How can *you* let your light shine?

**Property of
PROJECT ADELANTE**

La Rama

reloj de versos

©Derechos Reservados:

CIDCLI, S.C.
Centro de Información y Desarrollo
de la Comunicación y la Literatura Infantiles.
Av. México 145 - 601
Col. del Carmen Coyoacán
C.P. 04100, México, D.F.

Esta primera edición se coedita con la

Dirección General de Publicaciones
del Consejo Nacional para la Cultura y las Artes.

Primera edición, junio 1991.
ISBN 968-494-046-7

Impreso en México / *Printed in Mexico.*

Reproducción fotográfica: Pablo Esteva

Octavio Paz
La Rama
Ilustraciones de Tetsuo Kitora

CANTA en la punta del pino
un pájaro detenido,
trémulo, sobre su trino.

Se yergue, flecha, en la rama,
se desvanece entre alas
y en música se derrama.

El pájaro es una astilla
que canta y se quema viva
en una nota amarilla.

Alzo los ojos: no hay nada.
Silencio sobre la rama,
sobre la rama quebrada.

Viento

CANTAN las hojas,
bailan las peras en el peral;
gira la rosa,
rosa del viento, no del rosal.

Nubes y nubes
flotan dormidas, algas del aire;
todo el espacio
gira con ellas, fuerza de nadie.

 Todo es espacio;
vibra la vara de la amapola
y una desnuda
vuela en el viento lomo de ola.

Nada soy yo,
cuerpo que flota, luz, oleaje;
todo es del viento
y el viento es aire siempre de viaje.

La Rama se acabó de imprimir en el mes de septiembre de 1991, en los talleres de Editorial y Litografía Regina de los Ángeles, S.A. Avenida Trece 101-L, C.P. 03660, México, D.F. El tiraje fue de diez mil ejemplares.